# Pumpkin Hill

Appliqué a Whimsical Quilter's Tale

Anne Sutton

Martingale®
Create with Confidence

Pumpkin Hill: Appliqué a Whimsical Quilter's Tale
© 2020 by Anne Sutton

Martingale®
19021 120th Ave. NE, Ste. 102
Bothell, WA 98011-9511 USA
ShopMartingale.com

Printed in Hong Kong
25 24 23 22 21 20   8 7 6 5 4 3 2 1

Library of Congress Cataloging-in-Publication Data is available upon request.

ISBN: 978-1-68356-076-0

MISSION STATEMENT

We empower makers who use fabric and yarn to make life more enjoyable.

CREDITS

PUBLISHER AND
CHIEF VISIONARY OFFICER
Jennifer Erbe Keltner

CONTENT DIRECTOR
Karen Costello Soltys

DESIGN MANAGER
Adrienne Smitke

MANAGING EDITOR
Tina Cook

PRODUCTION MANAGER
Regina Girard

ACQUISITIONS AND
DEVELOPMENT EDITOR
Laurie Baker

COVER AND
BOOK DESIGNER
Mia Mar

TECHNICAL EDITOR
Carolyn Beam

LOCATION PHOTOGRAPHER
Adam Albright

COPY EDITOR
Sheila Chapman Ryan

STUDIO PHOTOGRAPHER
Brent Kane

ILLUSTRATOR
Sandy Loi

SPECIAL THANKS
Photography for this book was taken at Carol Hansen's Garden Barn in Indianola, Iowa.

Contents

Introduction
page 5

General Directions
page 6

Preface: Pumpkin Hill
page 12

Chapter 1: Double Acorns
page 14

Chapter 2: Pumpkin Coach
page 16

Chapter 3: Squirrel over the Moon
page 18

Chapter 4: Cottage on Pumpkin Hill
page 21

Chapter 5: Birds in the Pumpkin Patch
page 24

Chapter 6: Perched on a Pumpkin
page 27

Chapter 7: Basket o' Plenty
page 29

Chapter 8: Laurel Wreath
page 31

Chapter 9: Pumpkin Swag & Borders
page 33

Assembling the Quilt
page 34

About the Author
page 36

Introduction

Fall is in the air at Pumpkin Hill and the animals are busy getting ready for winter. Pumpkin Hill is a magical place that you can re-create in fabric and enjoy every fall; squirrels, birds, and a wise old owl make this quilt so much fun to appliqué. Add pumpkins galore, acorns, stars, and a sunflower, and soon you'll have your very own Pumpkin Hill.

This is not a quilt to rush through. Relax and enjoy the pleasure of appliqué. I hope you have as much fun making this quilt as I did. I wish you many happy hours of stitching!

~Anne

General Directions

For the best experience, read all instructions completely before beginning. Let's start with an overview of techniques and general tips.

Needle-turn and spray-starch appliqué are my favorite methods of appliqué, and I've designed this pattern with those techniques in mind. The quilt will work equally well with any appliqué method. Remember that if you prefer fusible appliqué, the template patterns have *not* been reversed.

You'll find basic directions for needle-turn appliqué and spray-starch appliqué on the following pages. If this is the first time you've tried appliqué, I suggest you take a class or purchase a good how-to book from your local quilt store. You can also visit ShopMartingale.com/HowtoQuilt to download free, illustrated appliqué instructions.

To make stems, use a ¼"-bias maker or bias bars. To use a bias maker, simply cut a ½"-wide bias strip for each stem and then follow the manufacturer's directions.

I don't prewash fabrics, because I like to work with the natural sizing in the fabric and find that appliqué motifs ravel less when unwashed.

When cutting and stitching, be as accurate as possible. The extra time and effort you spend will be well worth it. Note that pattern diagrams show unfinished sizes. Measure carefully before you cut and again after you sew the backgrounds together. If your measurements are off, this is the time to correct mistakes.

Needle-Turn Appliqué

Needle-turn appliqué gives a softer, more rounded look to appliqué. For needle-turn appliqué, I make templates from freezer paper.

Preparing the Appliqués

 Trace each pattern onto the dull side of freezer paper, leaving ½" between pieces. Don't add seam allowances. Cut out on the traced lines.

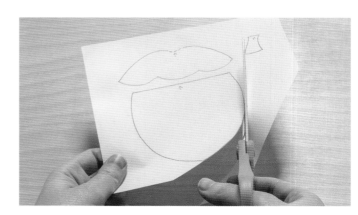

With a hot, dry iron, press the shiny side of the freezer-paper template to the right side of the appliqué fabric. The freezer paper will adhere to the fabric.

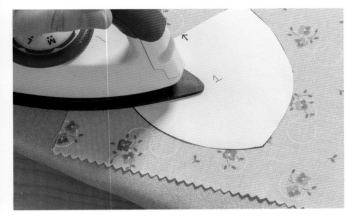

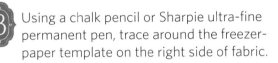 Using a chalk pencil or Sharpie ultra-fine permanent pen, trace around the freezer-paper template on the right side of fabric.

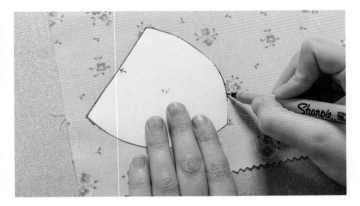

To make the shape easier to see, you can leave the freezer paper on the fabric until you are done cutting. Cut out the fabric approximately ¼" from the traced line.

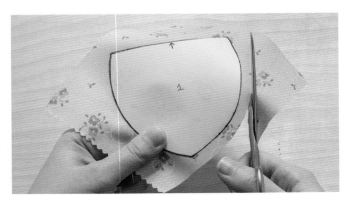

 Clip any inside curves up to the traced line. Remove the freezer paper.

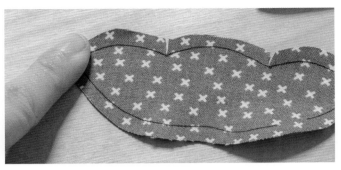

Perfect Placement

You may want to trace a few placement lines onto the front of your appliqué background to help with positioning the motifs. Using a light box or a bright window, trace the pattern onto the front of the appliqué background with a chalk pencil or a water-erasable marker.

Pin or glue baste your appliqué pieces to the background, starting with the bottommost layer.

Accommodating Tight Stitches

If you have a tendency to appliqué with tight tension, you can cut your backgrounds a little larger than called for and then trim to fit after appliquéing the motifs. I personally don't do this. I like to see exactly how my appliqué fits on the block, and I'm very careful not to pull my stitches too tight. But if you suspect that starting with oversized backgrounds will help you finish with accurately sized blocks, give it a try.

The Appliqué Stitch

1. Thread your needle with about 18" of a single strand of thread. It's easier to thread a needle if you cut the end of your thread at a slant.

2. Run your thread through some thread wax to help keep it from tangling.

3. Beginning on as straight an edge as possible, use the point of your needle to turn under the appliqué seam allowance, hiding the traced line. Turn only about ½" at a time.

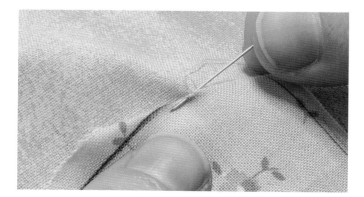

4. Holding the appliqué in place with your non-sewing hand, come up from the wrong side of the fabric and insert the needle into the folded edge of the seam allowance, barely catching the edge of your appliqué.

5. Your stitch should be invisible, so don't take a "bite" out of your appliqué piece. Make a tiny straight stitch by reentering the background right next to where your thread came up. If you're left-handed, stitch from left to right. If you're right-handed, stitch from right to left.

6. When you approach a curve or point, start making smaller stitches about ½" from the point. Come up from underneath right at the point but not into it. Use the tip of your needle to push any excess seam allowance under the point. Bring the thread into the point, give it a little tug to straighten the point, and go back into the background fabric. Continue down the next side.

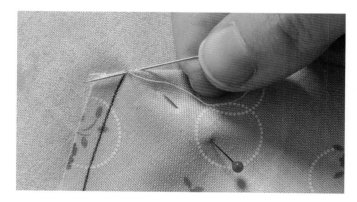

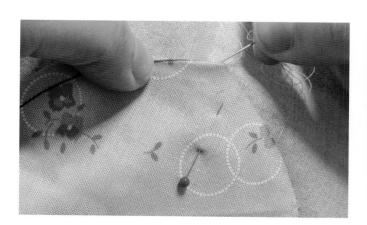

Spray-Starch Appliqué

The spray-starch method of appliqué gives the appliqué a crisp look and is a little easier for beginners. It also allows you the opportunity to see the entire block arranged on the background before you begin stitching.

Materials

- Spray starch or Mary Ellen's Best Press
- Sharpie ultra-fine black permanent pen
- Freezer paper
- Small, sharp embroidery scissors and paper scissors (curved scissors are also nice but not required)
- Stiletto or wood toothpick
- Glass jar with lid
- Small stencil brush or paintbrush
- Small craft iron
- Roxanne Glue-Baste-it

Instructions

 Using a black permanent pen, trace one of each appliqué shape onto the shiny side of freezer paper.

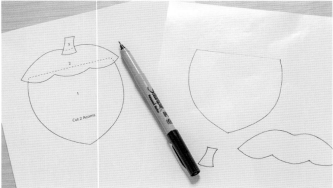

 Press the traced pattern, shiny side down, onto the dull side of another piece of freezer paper. You've just made a template sandwich with the traced line on the inside. This automatically reverses the image and you are ready to cut out your pattern pieces.

 Cut out all shapes on the traced lines. If you have a pair of curved scissors, use them to cut around the curves on the appliqué shapes (the smoother the edge of your appliqué shape, the smoother your finished appliqué will look). When cutting out your shapes, try turning the paper and not the scissors.

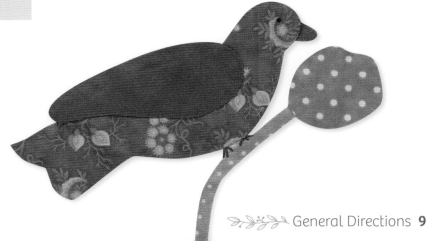

Press the shiny side of the appliqué templates to the wrong side of the appliqué fabric. Using sharp embroidery scissors, cut out each shape ¼" from the edge. Clip the inner curves almost to the traced line; stop just a few threads before the line. Don't worry about the outer curves. They don't need to be clipped.

Spray some starch into a container (preferably a small container with a lid; I use a baby-food jar). With your paintbrush, start in the center or straight edge of one edge of one appliqué shape and paint the starch onto the seam allowance. Keep the freezer paper in place and work with small sections (approximately 3").

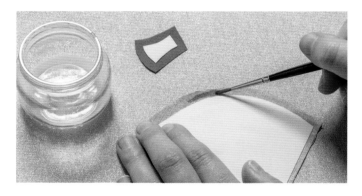

Using the point of your small craft iron (you can use a large iron, but it's much easier with a craft iron), press the seam allowance over onto the freezer paper. Use just the point of the iron and not the whole surface. Use a stiletto or a wood toothpick to "pull" your seam allowance onto the freezer paper. Continue around the shape until the entire seam allowance is pressed onto the freezer paper.

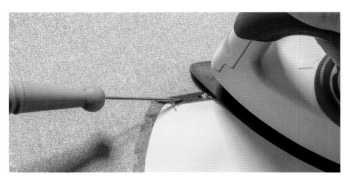

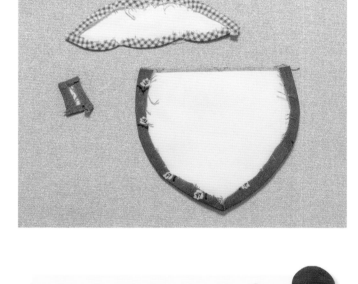

Pressing Matters

If you're right-handed, press from right to left. This will automatically point the corner "flags" in the right direction for appliqué. If you're left-handed, press from left to right around your shape.

7. To make the freezer paper easier to remove, turn your appliqué shape over and press from the top. Carefully remove the freezer paper. Save the freezer-paper shapes in a plastic bag after you remove them; you can reuse the shapes several times.

8. Place the pattern over a light box or on a table. Place the appliqué background fabric on top of the pattern. Using Roxanne Glue-Baste-It, draw a thin line of glue around the inside seam allowance of your appliqué shape. A fine line is preferable to little dots, since dots have a tendency to spread out when you place your shape on the appliqué fabric. Position the appliqué shapes on top of the background, starting with the bottommost layer. Appliqué the shapes using the appliqué stitch (page 8).

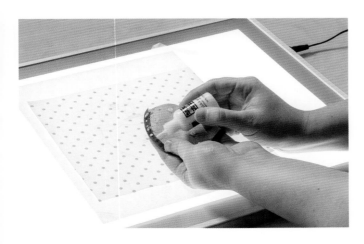

Embroidery

Transfer all embroidery lines to the fabric before beginning to appliqué. Place the pattern over a light box or bright window and trace the embroidery details with a fine-point water-erasable marker or a fabric pencil.

The key to good embroidery is *tiny* stitches. Use two strands of embroidery floss and keep your stitches as even and as small as possible. Don't pull the thread too tightly or it will disappear into the fabric and distort the piece.

Only four embroidery stitches are required for the entire quilt: backstitch, French knot, satin stitch, and stem stitch.

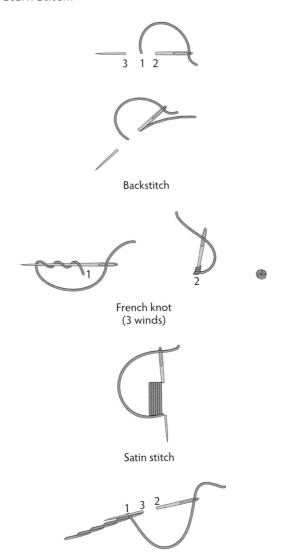

Backstitch

French knot
(3 winds)

Satin stitch

Stem stitch

Pumpkin Hill

Materials

Yardage is based on 42"-wide fabric. Fat quarters measure 18" × 21".

Background and Appliqués

- 4 fat quarters of assorted olive prints for acorn, grass, squirrel collars, and patchwork

- 4 fat quarters of assorted dark brown prints or solids for acorn caps, beaks, squirrels, roof, and pumpkin door

- 10 fat quarters of assorted cream prints for background

- 1 fat quarter of tan floral for patchwork, dormer, and pumpkin vine

- 1 fat quarter of yellow dot for moon, windows, and patchwork

- 3 fat quarters of assorted reds for pumpkins, birds, heart, house, chimneys, berries, and stars

- 4 fat quarters of assorted apricot prints for background, flower petals, dormer, acorns, and pumpkins

- 3 fat quarters of assorted peach prints for pumpkins and flower center

- 5 fat quarters of assorted medium brown prints for background, patchwork, squirrels, baskets, pumpkin wheels, house door, window frames, stars, sunflower center, acorn, leaves, flower, stems, and owl

- ½ yard *each* of cream print and marbled butterscotch print for background, pumpkin windows, owl eyes, and owl beak

- ½ yard *each* of 2 green prints for vines, sunflower stems, and leaves

- ½ yard of marbled orange print for pumpkins

Borders, Binding, and Backing

- ½ yard of medium brown floral for inner border

- 1 yard of honey print for outer border

- 1⅓ yards of apricot check for top garland

- 1 yard of brown check for bias binding*

- 3¾ yards of fabric for backing

- 64" × 72" piece of batting

*If you prefer straight-cut binding, you'll need ½ yard.

Embroidery and Embellishments

- Water-erasable marker or chalk pencil

- 5"-wide embroidery hoop

- 1 skein *each* of DMC embroidery floss in #838 brown, #732 green, and #310 black

- Embroidery needle in size #8, #10, or #11

- 2 flower buttons, 1" diameter, for coach wheels

- 1 star button, ½" diameter, for coach door

- 1 button, ½" diameter, for house doorknob

Appliqué Supplies

- Size #10 or #11 appliqué needle

- Appliqué thread to match fabric (I like Aurifil 80 weight)

- Appliqué pins

- Fabric-basting glue (such as Roxanne Glue-Baste-It)

- Freezer paper

- Chalk pencil and ultra-fine permanent marker

- Small, sharp appliqué scissors and paper scissors

- Clover ¼"-bias maker or bias bars

- Spray starch (optional)

Finished size: 57½" × 65½"

Designed by Anne Sutton; quilted by Lynne Todoroff;
and appliquéd by my wonderful friends. Thank you!

Double Acorns

What You Need

All measurements include ¼" seam allowances.

- 2 different 6½" × 6½" squares: 1 cream print (A) and 1 apricot print (B)
- 1 medium brown print strip, 1½" × 12½" (C)
- 1 cream print strip, 1½" × 7½" (D)
- 1 cream print strip, 1½" × 13½" (E)
- 1 medium brown print strip, 1½" × 8½" (F)

Preparing the Appliqués

Using the Double Acorns patterns on pattern sheet 3 and referring to "General Directions" on page 6, cut and prepare the appliqué shapes.

Making the Double Acorns Section

Press seam allowances as indicated by the arrows.

 Join squares A and B to make a rectangle. Sew strip C to the right edge. In alphabetical order, sew D to the top, E to the left, and F to the bottom to make a background unit that measures 8½"×14½", including seam allowances.

 Center one acorn on square A and one on square B. Pin or glue baste. Referring to "General Directions," appliqué the acorns, caps, and stems using your favorite method.

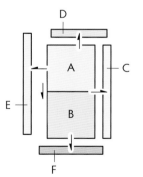

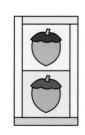

Double Acorns section, 8½" × 14½"

Pumpkin Coach

What You Need

All measurements include ¼" seam allowances.

- 1 cream print square, 10½" × 10½" (G)
- 1 apricot print strip, 4½" × 14½" (H)
- 1 cream print strip, 6½" × 14½" (I)
- 2 yellow dot squares, 4½" × 4½" (J)
- 2 cream print squares, 4½" × 4½" (K)
- 1 butterscotch strip, 4½" × 8½" (L)

Preparing the Appliqués

Using the Pumpkin Coach patterns on pattern sheet 1 and referring to "General Directions" on page 6, cut and prepare the appliqué shapes. Placing the patterns and appliqué shapes over a light box or bright window, use a water-erasable marker or chalk pencil to trace the squirrels' eyes and the lines for the windowpanes.

Assembling the Pumpkin Coach Section

 Join rectangles H and I. Sew the G square to the left edge. Join a J square and a K square, then add rectangle L to the right side. Join the remaining J and K squares and sew them to the right of the L rectangle, checking that the squares are in the correct order. Sew this unit to the bottom edge of G/H/I to make a background unit that measures 14½" × 24½", including seam allowances.

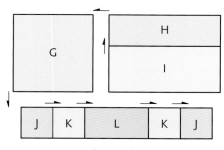

Background unit,
14½" × 24½"

 Referring to the photo on page 16, position all the appliqué shapes *except* the leaves on the background and glue baste. Position the coach's wheels and the legs of one squirrel just above the seam of the star row. Do not cover the seam. Baste, then appliqué. Position the stars on rectangle L and the J squares. Baste, then appliqué.

Adding Embroidery and Leaves

Use two strands of floss for embroidery.

 Embroider the windowpanes with brown floss and a stem stitch. Using black floss, outline the eyes with a tiny backstitch and fill them in with a satin stitch.

 Using the Pumpkin Coach patterns on pattern sheet 1, trace the vines onto the background. Using brown floss, embroider the vines with a stem stitch. Referring to the photo, position, baste, and appliqué the leaves to complete the Pumpkin Coach section.

Joining the Sections

Sew the Pumpkin Coach section to the right edge of the Double Acorns section (page 15). The joined sections should measure 14½" × 32½", including seam allowances.

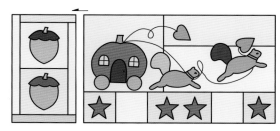

14½" × 32½"

Squirrel over the Moon

What You Need

All measurements include ¼" seam allowances.

- 1 cream marble square, 10½" × 10½" (A)
- 11 assorted squares, 2½" × 2½": 3 cream prints, 2 olive prints, 3 apricot prints, 2 medium brown prints, and 1 butterscotch marble (B)
- 1 cream print rectangle, 2½" × 12½" (C)

Preparing the Appliqués

 Using the Squirrel over the Moon patterns on pattern sheet 4 and referring to "General Directions" on page 6, cut and prepare the appliqué shapes.

 Placing the patterns and appliqué shapes over a light box or bright window, use a water-erasable marker or chalk pencil to trace the embroidery lines for the squirrel's eye and owl's eyes.

Assembling the Squirrel over the Moon Section

Press seam allowances as indicated by the arrows.

 Randomly join five B squares. Sew the pieced squares to the left edge of the A square. Join six B squares and sew them to the bottom edge of A/B. Sew the C rectangle to the bottom edge to make a background unit that measures 12½" × 14½", including seam allowances.

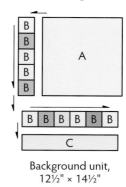

Background unit,
12½" × 14½"

2. Referring to the photo on page 18, position the appliqué shapes on the background and side squares and glue baste. Do not cover the seam allowance. Referring to "General Directions," appliqué the pieces using your favorite method.

3. Trace the embroidery lines for the owl's feet after placing the owl on the moon (if you can't see through the fabric to trace, you can freehand draw three lines for each foot).

Adding Embroidery

Use two strands of floss for embroidery. Embroider the owl's feet with black floss and a tiny stem stitch. Use black floss to outline the squirrel and owl eyes with a tiny backstitch and fill them in with a satin stitch.

Cottage on Pumpkin Hill

Preparing the Appliqués

Using the Cottage on Pumpkin Hill patterns on pattern sheets 1 and 2 and referring to "General Directions" on page 6, cut and prepare the appliqué shapes.

Assembling the Background

Press seam allowances as indicated by the arrows.

 Sew A to the left edge of C. Sew B to the left edge of D. Join the units to make a background unit that measures 14½" × 24½", including seam allowances.

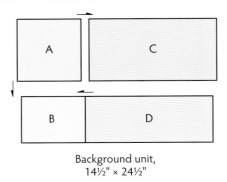

Background unit,
14½" × 24½"

 Join the eight H rectangles, alternating colors, to make a grass unit that measures 6" × 24½", including seam allowances.

 Cut a piece of freezer paper 26" long. Place the freezer paper over the grass pattern (pattern sheet 2) and trace. Use the freezer-paper template to cut the grass unit from the H rectangles.

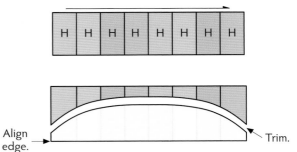

 Aligning the bottom and side edges, appliqué the top edge of the grass unit to the background.

What You Need

All measurements include ¼" seam allowances.

- 1 cream print square, 8½" × 8½" (A)
- 1 cream print strip, 6½" × 8½" (B)
- 1 cream print strip, 8½" × 16½" (C)
- 1 cream print strip, 6½" × 16½" (D)
- 3 cream print squares, 4½" × 4½" (E)
- 6 squares, 2⅞" × 2⅞", in matching pairs: 2 olive print, 2 medium brown print, and 2 apricot print. Cut each square in half diagonally to yield 12 triangles total (F).
- 3 cream print squares, 3⅜" × 3⅜" (G)
- 8 assorted olive print rectangles, 3½" × 6", in 4 matching pairs (H)

Appliquéing the House, Flower, and Pumpkin

 Referring to the photo on page 21, center the house on the grass, with the bottom of the house covering about ⅛" of grass. Glue baste, then appliqué the house pieces in place, starting with the bottommost layer.

 Using a green print and the ¼"-bias maker or bias bars, follow the manufacturer's instructions to make a 20" length of ¼"-wide bias stem. Place the main stem approximately 4½" from the left edge. Line up the bottom of the stem with the bottom of the background. Position the smaller stems, leaves, and flower. Baste, then appliqué in place, starting with the bottommost layer.

 Position the pumpkins approximately 3" from the right edge and 2¼" from the bottom raw edge. Baste, then appliqué in place, starting with the bottommost layer.

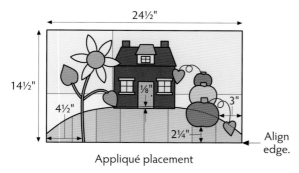

Appliqué placement

 Place the pattern and block over a light box or a bright window. Trace the embroidery lines for the windowpanes and pumpkin vines onto the background fabric using a water-erasable marker. Position and appliqué the pumpkin leaves.

Adding Embroidery

Use two strands of floss for embroidery. Embroider the vines with green floss and a tiny stem stitch. Embroider the windowpanes with brown floss and a stem stitch.

Adding the Diamond Units

 Select one G square and four matching F triangles. Sew F triangles to opposite edges of G. Sew F triangles to the remaining edges to make a diamond unit that measures 4½" square, including seam allowances. Make three diamond units.

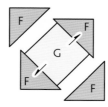

Make 3 units,
4½" × 4½".

 Join three diamond units and three E squares, alternating them. Sew this strip to the top of the house unit to complete the Cottage on Pumpkin Hill section, which should measure 18½" × 24½", including seam allowances.

18½" × 24½"

Birds in the Pumpkin Patch

What You Need

All measurements include ¼" seam allowances.

- 1 cream print square, 8½" × 8½" (A)
- 1 cream print rectangle, 6½" × 7½" (B)
- 6 squares, 2½" × 2½": 2 matching cream print, 1 different cream print, 1 butterscotch marble, 1 olive print, and 1 yellow dot (C)
- 1 apricot print rectangle, 2½" × 3½" (D)
- 1 cream print rectangle, 6½" × 8½" (E)
- 1 apricot print rectangle, 6½" × 9½" (F)
- 3 strips, 1½" × 14½": 1 cream print, 1 butterscotch marble, and 1 olive print (G)
- 4 squares, 2⅞" × 2⅞": 2 matching cream print and 2 matching apricot print. Cut each square in half diagonally to yield 8 triangles total (H).
- 1 olive print square, 3⅜" × 3⅜" (I)
- 1 medium brown square, 3⅜" × 3⅜" (I)
- 12 squares, 2⅞" × 2⅞": 2 matching cream print, 2 different matching cream print, 2 yellow dot, 2 matching apricot print, 2 matching medium brown print, and 2 tan floral. Cut each square in half diagonally to yield 24 triangles total (J).

Preparing the Appliqués

Using the Birds in the Pumpkin Patch patterns on pattern sheet 2 and referring to "General Directions" on page 6, cut and prepare the appliqué shapes.

Assembling the Birds in the Pumpkin Patch Section

Press seam allowances as indicated by the arrows.

 Join three C squares and sew them to the right edge of B. Join the remaining three C squares and sew the D rectangle to the left edge; sew to the bottom edge of B/C. Sew this unit to the right edge of A.

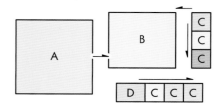

 Join E to the left edge of F and join to the bottom of the step 1 unit. Sew the butterscotch G to the left edge, followed by the cream G, and then the olive G to make a background unit that measures 14½" × 20½", including seam allowances.

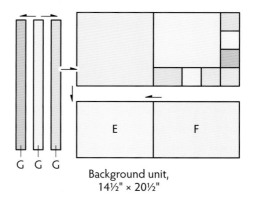

Background unit,
14½" × 20½"

 Center the flying bird and basket on piece B. Pin or glue baste. Referring to the photo on page 24, position the remaining appliqué shapes. Baste, then appliqué in place, starting with the bottommost layer.

 Place the pattern and block over a light box or a bright window. Trace the embroidery lines for the basket handle, twigs and bird legs, feet and eyes using a water-erasable marker.

Adding Embroidery

Use two strands of floss for embroidery.

 For the flying bird, embroider the basket handle and twigs with brown floss and a stem stitch. Then embroider the bird's eye with black floss and a French knot.

 For the bird on the pumpkin, embroider the feet and legs with brown floss and a stem stitch. Use black floss to outline the eye with a tiny backstitch and fill it in with a satin stitch.

Adding the Diamond and Pinwheel Units

 Select one I square and four matching H triangles. Sew H triangles to opposite edges of I. Sew H triangles to the remaining edges to make a diamond unit that measures 4½" square, including seam allowances. Make two diamond units.

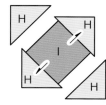

Make 2 units,
4½" × 4½".

 Select one set of four matching light J triangles and one set of four matching medium J triangles. Sew a light and medium J together to make a half-square-triangle unit. Make four.

Make 4 units,
2½" × 2½".

 Arrange the units in two rows. Sew the units into rows; join the rows to make a pinwheel unit that measures 4½" square, including seam allowances. Make three pinwheel units.

Make 3 units,
4½" × 4½".

 Join three pinwheel units and two diamond units, alternating them. Sew to the bottom of the background unit to complete the Birds in the Pumpkin Patch section, which should measure 18½" × 20½", including seam allowances.

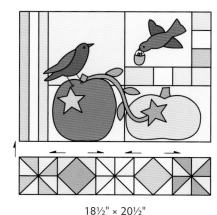

18½" × 20½"

Perched on a Pumpkin

What You Need

All measurements include ¼" seam allowances.

- 2 cream print squares, 6½" × 6½" (A)
- 1 butterscotch marble rectangle, 6½" × 12½" (B)
- 13 squares, 2½" × 2½": 2 matching cream print, 4 assorted cream prints, 1 yellow dot, 3 assorted medium brown prints, 2 matching apricot prints, and 1 different apricot print (C)

Preparing the Appliqués

Using the Perched on a Pumpkin patterns on pattern sheet 4 and referring to "General Directions" on page 6, cut and prepare the appliqué shapes.

Assembling the Perched on a Pumpkin Section

Press seam allowances as indicated by the arrows.

 Join the two A squares to make a rectangle. Join six C squares and sew them to the top edge of the A squares. Join B to the bottom edge of the A squares. Join seven C squares and sew them to the right edge to make a background unit that measures 14½" square, including seam allowances.

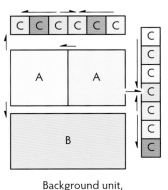

**Background unit,
14½" × 14½"**

 Using a green print and the ¼"-bias maker or bias bars, follow the manufacturer's instructions to make an 18" length of ¼"-wide bias vine.

 Referring to the photo on page 27, position the appliqué shapes on the background. Baste, then appliqué in place, starting with the bottommost layer.

4 Place the pattern and background over a light box or a bright window. Trace the stems, the bird's feet, and the bird's eye.

Adding Embroidery

Use two strands of floss for embroidery. Embroider the leaf stems with green floss and a stem stitch, the bird's feet with brown floss and a tiny stem stitch, and the bird's eye with black floss and a French knot.

Basket o' Plenty

Preparing the Appliqués

Using the Basket o' Plenty patterns on pattern sheet 3 and referring to "General Directions" on page 6, cut and prepare the appliqué shapes.

Assembling the Basket o' Plenty Section

Press seam allowances as indicated by the arrows.

1. Join square A to the left edge of rectangle B. Sew rectangle C to the bottom edge and then sew rectangle D to the left edge. Join the two E rectangles and sew them to the right edge. Join the two F strips and sew them to the top edge to make a background unit that measures 14½" × 18½", including seam allowances.

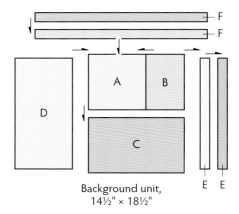

Background unit,
14½" × 18½"

What You Need

All measurements include ¼" seam allowances.

- 1 cream print square, 6½" × 6½" (A)
- 1 apricot print rectangle, 4½" × 6½" (B)
- 1 olive print rectangle, 6½" × 10½" (C)
- 1 cream marble rectangle, 6½" × 12½" (D)
- 1 cream print rectangle, 1½" × 12½" (E)
- 1 olive print rectangle, 1½" × 12½" (E)
- 2 strips, 1½" × 18½": 1 butterscotch marble and 1 medium brown print (F)

2. Referring to the photo on page 29, position the appliqué shapes (except for the leaf) on the background. Baste, then appliqué in place, starting with the bottommost layer.

3. Place the pattern and background over a light box or a bright window. Trace the pumpkin-vine embroidery line and the squirrel's eye using a water-erasable marker. Appliqué the leaf at the end of the vine.

Adding Embroidery

Use two strands of floss for embroidery. Embroider the vine with green floss and a stem stitch. Use black floss to outline the eye with a tiny backstitch and fill it in with a satin stitch.

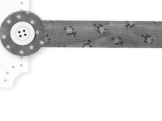

Laurel Wreath

What You Need

All measurements include ¼" seam allowances.

- 6 squares, 2½" × 2½": 1 medium brown, 1 apricot print, and 4 assorted cream prints (A)
- 1 cream print square, 12½" × 12½" (B)

Preparing the Appliqués

 Using the Laurel Wreath patterns on pattern sheet 3 and referring to "General Directions" on page 6, cut and prepare the appliqué shapes.

 Using a green print and the ¼"-bias maker or bias bars, follow the manufacturer's instructions to make a 22" length of ¼"-wide bias vine.

 Placing the pattern and background over a light box or bright window, use a water-erasable marker or chalk pencil to trace a thin placement line for the vine.

Assembling the Laurel Wreath Section

Press seam allowances as indicated by the arrows.

 Join the A squares. Stitch the pieced A squares to the top edge of B to make a background unit

that measures 12½" × 14½", including seam allowances.

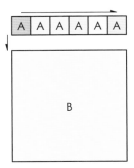

Background unit, 12½" × 14½"

 Referring to the photo on page 31, position the appliqué on the background. Baste, then appliqué in place, starting with the bottommost layer. Appliqué the berries and acorns after the wreath and squirrel are complete.

Adding Embroidery

Place the pattern and background over a light box or a bright window. Trace the squirrel's eye. Use two strands of floss for embroidery. Use black floss to outline the squirrel's eye with a tiny backstitch and fill it in with a satin stitch.

Pumpkin Swag & Borders

What You Need

All measurements include ¼" seam allowances.

From the apricot check, cut on the *lengthwise* grain:
1 strip, 6½" × 44½"*

From the medium brown floral, cut:
5 strips, 2½" × 42"

From the honey print, cut:
6 strips, 5" × 42"

From the brown check, cut:
2½"-wide bias strips to total 254"**

If cutting on the crosswise grain, cut 2 strips, 6½" × 42", and piece end to end. Trim to 44½" long.

**If you prefer non-bias binding, cut 7 strips, 2½" × the width of fabric.*

Preparing the Appliqués

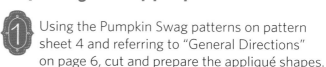

1. Using the Pumpkin Swag patterns on pattern sheet 4 and referring to "General Directions" on page 6, cut and prepare the appliqué shapes.

2. Using a green print and the ¼"-bias maker or bias bars, follow the manufacturer's instructions to make two 17" lengths of ¼"-wide bias vines.

3. Placing the pattern and background over a light box or bright window, use a water-erasable marker or chalk pencil to trace the vine placement and embroidery lines for the heart string and leaf tendrils, tracing from the center outward. Trace one side, then flip the pattern and trace the other side.

Adding Appliqué and Embroidery

Position the appliqué on the background. Baste, then appliqué. Embroider the vine tendrils with brown floss and a stem stitch. Embroider the heart string with green floss and a stem stitch.

Assembling the Quilt

Press seam allowances as indicated by the arrows.

 Referring to the diagram below, join the sections. The quilt center should measure 44½" × 52½", including seam allowances.

 Sew the medium brown floral strips together end to end. Cut this strip into two lengths, 52½" long, and sew to opposite sides of the quilt center. Cut two lengths, 48½" long, and sew to the top and bottom.

 Sew the honey strips together end to end. Cut this strip into two lengths, 56½" long, and sew to opposite sides of the quilt top. Cut two lengths, 57½" long, and sew to the top and bottom. The quilt top should measure 57½" × 65½".

Quilt assembly

Layering and Quilting

Layer the quilt top with batting and backing; baste. Hand or machine quilt. In the quilt shown:

- Double Acorns is quilted with crosshatching in the acorns
- Pumpkin Coach is quilted with hearts and loops in the coach
- Squirrel over the Moon is quilted with stars and loops, with curves in the pieced squares
- Cottage on Pumpkin Hill is quilted with a teardrop meander, with wavy lines in the grass
- Birds in the Pumpkin Patch and Perched on a Pumpkin are quilted with a leafy meander, with curves in the diamond units and pieced squares and swirls in the pinwheel units
- Basket o' Plenty is quilted with swirls
- Laurel Wreath is quilted with loops
- The appliqué is ditch and outline quilted
- The inner border is quilted with a braid
- The outer border is quilted with flowers and leaves

Binding and Buttons

1. Use the brown check 2½"-wide bias strips to make the binding, and then sew the binding to the quilt.

2. Sew the flower buttons to the coach wheels and the star button to the coach door in the Double Acorns section. Sew the remaining button to the house door in the Cottage on Pumpkin Hill section.

About the Author

Sweet sophistication with a touch of whimsy. That's the tagline of Anne Sutton's company, Bunny Hill Designs, and that's the look her fans adore in her quilt patterns and in the prints she designs for Moda Fabrics. Anne has always loved sewing and crafts, especially appliqué, which speaks to her as no other craft has. She spends her days surrounded by pets in her Northern California loft studio. You can visit Anne at BunnyHillDesigns.com.